Caring for tulsi

om premavatara vidmahe
satguru devaya dhimahi
thanno vishwananda prachodayath

This book is dedicated to our beloved Guruji

Sri Swami Vishwananda

ISBN 978-3-940381-30-9

index

introduction

Ya Drsta Nikhila Agha Sangha Shamani Sprsta Vapuh Pavani
Roganam Abhivandita Nirasini Siktantaka Trasini
Pratya Satti Vidhayini Bhagavataha Krshnasya Samropita
Nyasta Tacharane Vimukti Phalada Tasmyai Tulasyai Namah

Just by looking at You (Tulsi), all sins become removed. Just by touching You, one's body becomes pure. By praying to You, all diseases become removed. If one waters You or makes You wet, the fear of death is destroyed. Just by planting or transplanting, one achieves nearness to The Lord. If someone offers Your leaf to the lotus feet of Narayanaya, You award liberation and devotion to them; therefore I pay my humble respects to such a wonderful Tulsi Devi.

Yanmule Sarva Thirthani Yanmadye Sarva Devatha
Yadagre Sarva Vedashcha Tulsi Twam Namam Mayham

At Tulsi's base (roots or feet) are all the holy places, in Her middle portion (stems or body) are all the Devas and Devis and in Her top portion (leaves or head) reside all the Vedas. To You I humbly bow.

In these two prayers we can see the greatness of Tulsi Devi. Even though Tulsi is Divine Mother Herself, out of Her infinite mercy and joy to help Her children, She incarnates as a plant.

By observing the Tulsi plant we can learn many spiritual lessons. The first being humility. Tulsi is the Queen of the Universe. No amount of gold or jewels offered to Her could ever be enough to warrant the blessing of being near to Her. Yet She decided to subjugate Herself to the services of those who plant Her. Some of course do everything within their power to serve Her, and some do not, neglecting to see Her Divine Nature inside the plant. Ultimately She does not care, for even watering Her once is enough to firmly place you on the path of Self-realization, such is Her Love.

The story of Tulsi in short

From a curse placed on his grandfather, King Dharmadhvaja did many penances to please Lakshmi. Lakshmi was very pleased with his devotion and incarnated as his daughter. They named Her Tulsi, for Her beauty was incomparable with any other in creation.

Soon after Her birth, however, Tulsi ran off to Badrinath and practicesd severe austerities for 100,000 years with the ultimate goal of attaining Lord Narayana as Her Husband. When She completed Her austerities Brahma appeared and granted Her wish. But unbeknownst to Tulsi, Narayana had also partially incarnated as a demon king, Sankhschuda. Sankhschuda also did many years of austerities to attain Tulsi as his wife. Lord Brahma being pleased with him granted his desire, also. For thousands of years, Tulsi was happily the wife of the demon king Sankhschuda.

Through Her one pointed Love for Her husband and Her unshakable Faith in Her Lord Narayana, Her husband was invincible. No one could kill him. War after war he came home victorious. Of course, he began to think his power came from himself, not the ceaseless payers of Tulsi.

With such pride in his mind, he attacked the Devas. They were easily overpowered. In fear they ran to Shiva for assistance. He agreed and sent His armies out to destroy Sankhschuda. All failed, even Muruga and Kali. Finally Shiva entered the fight, but before He was about to throw His trident, Narayana appeared to Him and asked Shiva to postpone the fight for one day.

"This evening," Narayana said, "I will enter Tulsi's chambers and take Her chastity."

As promised, Narayana appeared to Tulsi that evening, not in His true form, but in the guise of Sankhschuda. Tulsi was over joyed to see Her husband back from thousands of years of war. In Her excitement She was unable to see through Narayana's maya.

They spent the night enjoying themselves and in the morning when they awoke, Narayana left the bed in a very cold fashion. Her beloved husband would never do such a thing. Tulsi knew this was not Her husband.

"Who are you?! How dare you come to me in the form of my husband. Turn around and show me who you are."

Narayana turned around and showed Tulsi His true form. This was not enough to passify Her. For Tulsi knew that He came to Her so that Sankhschuda could be killed.

In Her furry She cursed Narayana, "As your heart is as cold as a stone, so I curse you to be a stone!"

Out of His endless Love for His devotee and the pain He felt for

deceiving His most dear and beloved Tulsi, He accepted the curse. Immediately His body turned to stone.
The universe went into chaos. And as Lakshmi lost Her Husband, She appeared to Tulsi dressed in white (the traditional color of widows in Hinduism). As Tulsi had just lost Her husband, She did not want to be the cause of another woman's pain, so She took back Her curse.

In Her agony, Tulsi burnt Herself to ash using Her own Shakti. After leaving Her body, She forgot the pains of the human life and merged with Her beloved Lord, Narayana.

Narayana knew the power of Tulsi's Bhakti, and knew that the universe and its inhabitants would need Her to incarnate on Earth as a basil plant, so that everyone could worship Her and by Her grace attain the Divine. He also added that since She would also stay on Earth, so would He. He took the form of the saligram (black stones) so that, "I may always sit below you."

So you can see, Tulsi is the epitome of faith and bhakti. And it is Her greatest joy to bless Her children with the same type of faith and bhakti.

In Her boundless mercy She accepted Narayana's request and continuously incarnates as a plant so that anyone can serve Her. One does not need special initiations or mantras. All one needs to serve Her as a plant to the best of their ability. This is more than sufficient to gain Her Grace.

The only prerequisite is that one needs to be vegetarian to serve Tulsi, as She is Divine Mother Herself, and all the animals are also Her children. Obviously a mother does not want her children to eat one another.

If you want to serve Tulsi, please remember this one rule.

caring for tulsi

Truly the most important thing needed to take care of Tulsi is Love. Love Her. Remember She appears to be a plant, however She is not. She is the Queen of the Universe and your Mother. Treat Her with respect and tenderness and She will treat you similarly a thousand times more.

The following sections on how to care for Tulsi are suggestions to support you in caring for Her. The word suggestions was used very carefully as Tulsi has grown happily and strong under all different kinds of conditions; much light & little light; much water & little water; unglazed pots & glazed pots; high humidity & low humidity; etc. The only constant variable was Love. Remember this. It is very important.

Varieties of Tulsi

There are three main varieties of Tulsi; Vana, Rama and Krishna Tulsi. Vana Tulsi has large green leaves with purple flowers. Rama Tulsi has smaller, lighter coloured, leaves with white flowers. And Krishna Tulsi has medium sized purple leaves with purple flowers.

Caring for all three types is virtually the same. The only major difference between these three are their growth speeds. The following sections are applicable for all three varieties.

Planting Tulsi from Seeds

Growing Tulsi from a seed can be difficult for some, though the great satisfaction of watching Her grow under your care from a baby to a bush is worth it. The best time to begin germinating Tulsi is in spring, however, if you plan to grow Her primarily indoors with artificial lights, you can plant Her anytime of the year.

To germinate Tulsi place Her seeds on top of the soil. The soil should be 1.5 to 2 inches deep (3.5 to 5 cm). If you plan to germinate more than one seed, place each seed at least 3 inches apart (7.5 cm). This will make it easier to transplant Her without hurting Her.

If this is your first Tulsi, it is recommended to grow only one, as She can be much work if She becomes sick.

Place clear cling wrap over the pot so that the moisture stays inside. Keep the soil semi moist. Mist the seeds with a spray bottle, this will help Her get the water She needs without disturbing the seeds.

It takes 10 to 14 days for Tulsi to germinate. Especially before She has germinated and up until Her second set of leaves have grown, it is best not to move Her too much (unless you need to turn Her so that She grows straight). After the first misting, Her seeds should not be disturbed as She may not germinate.

When She has grown Her second or third set of leaves, you may transplant Her.

Germinating Tulsi in peat moss cups will help you in caring for Her when She needs to be transplanted for the first time. Tulsi likes the peat moss cups as when placed in soil it deteriorates and turns into food for Tulsi. It also allows Her roots to come through when She is ready while protecting Her original root ball.

If you are using peat moss cups, when transplanting Tulsi, simply place the entire cup in the soil, making sure to keep the soil line of the cup and the pot the same. Otherwise watering problems may occur.

Where to place Tulsi

If you live in a climate that allows Tulsi to live outside all year around, plant Her anywhere outside.
If you live in a climate that allows Tulsi to live outside all year around, plant Her anywhere outside. If you live in a colder climate, the best place to keep Tulsi is in your prayer room. If this is not an adequate place, and you live in the northern hemisphere, try to find a south facing window. If you live in the southern hemisphere, place Tulsi in a north facing window.

If none of the above are appropriate, then place Her in a space where She will be respected. The only two rooms of the house which Tulsi should not be placed is the bedroom or bathroom.

Pot Size and Type

When choosing a pot to grow your Tulsi remember three things: make sure it has a drainage hole, it is large enough and that it is an unglazed clay pot (terracotta).

1. Drainage Hole
It is important that there is a drainage hole at the bottom of Tulsi's pot. This easily allows any excessive water to leave Her soil. If Tulsi's soil is too wet for an extended period of time, She will become sick (the ends of Her leaves begin to dry) and there is a chance that fungus develops on Her roots.

To keep the soil from being washed away through the drainage hole, you can place a stone or two to cover, but not plug, the hole. Or use a broken piece of another plant pot.

2. Size of the pot

The size of the pot Tulsi is in is very important, but easy to take care of. When Tulsi gets a large amount of room for Her roots to spread out, She is very happy and healthy, and it supports Her overall growth. Basically big pot = big Tulsi. If you do not have so much space for a large Tulsi, then it is okay to keep Her in a smaller pot for longer than is suggested. However if Tulsi is kept in a too small of a pot for too long, She will become sick (Her leaves begin to yellow & wilt, and Her natural immunity to pests will decrease).

Obviously we want a pot that fits Her age and size. I.e., if Tulsi is a seedling, we want a small pot for seedlings, however if Tulsi is given adequate light, water and room to grow, She can quickly grow to be 30 inches (80 cm) tall and 25 inches (63 cm) wide by the end of Her first Summer!

This is an example of an earthen pot.

The way to determine what is the next size large is, is to buy a pot that is 1 inch (2.5 cm) bigger in all dimensions. If Tulsi is getting adequate lighting, then She will most likely outgrow this pot very soon (1 to two months). So it is okay to get a pot which is 2 to 3 sizes larger. However, you need to make sure She is not being over watered.

3. Unglazed clay pot (terracotta)

Buying an unglazed earthen (or clay) pot (aka terracotta) is very important. This will help you be more sure of when Tulsi needs to be watered. The natural clay allows air to move through the sides of the pot which dries out the soil. This is very beneficial and important.
If you plant Tulsi in a glazed pot, Her soil will not dry out fast enough below the surface. This may lead to over watering and sickness (fungi, pests, drying of leaves, etc.).

Soil

The type of soil you plant Tulsi in obviously very important, but like most things it is very easy to get the right kind. You may also buy fertilizers to help Her grow.

1. Tulsi likes rich black soil; the same type of soil that is used in vegetable gardens. You can get this at any garden store. Make sure however, that this soil does not retain too much water. If this soil does, add sand. This will help with drainage and will allow air to pass through the soil drying it out.

2. Tulsi will of course use up the nutrients in the soil so you will need to get some type of fertilizer. There are so many different types and brands. Go to your local garden shop and tell them you have basil in a pot and that you want a natural or organic fertilizer (make sure not to buy fertilizer that have animal byproducts in them; e.g. fish emulsion). Whatever they give you should do the trick. Read the instruction carefully and do as recommended.

Water

When watering Tulsi we need to remember two things, how much and the quality of water.

1. When someone new takes care of Tulsi, they always ask, "How much should I water Her?" This is an simple question which could easily create a very complex answer. But let's try to keep it short and simple: Water Tulsi when She is thirsty.

Tulsi will need different amounts of water through the year and even from week to week or day to day. The amount of water She drinks is dependent on many variables (e.g. temperature, humidity, how much She is growing, amount of light). So the best and easiest way to know if She needs water is if She is a bit wilty. Of course, Tulsi Devi can wilt for many other reasons, however if you are taking care of Her well, it is most likely lack of water.

Letting Tulsi wilt before every watering is not nice for Her or you (it can even slowdown Her speed of growth and get Her sick), so what else to do? Touch Her leaves. Every day the first thing you should do is touch Tulsi Devi's leaves. This has immense spiritual benefit (see the section on benefit of caring for Tulsi Devi) and it will allow you to see when She needs water. If Her leaves are firm, strong and healthy, then She does not need water. If Her leaves are soft and clammy then She will need water later today or tomorrow. If Her leaves are visibly wilted, then she needs water now (if all of Her other needs are met).

Once you get the feeling for this, it is the easiest way to see how your Tulsi is doing.

As a side note: Touching Her leaves every day physically connects you and Her and will help immensely in connecting to Her (which is the whole reason for taking care of Her!).

2. The best water to use for Tulsi would be from a fresh, natural stream or pond, but this is difficult to come by. So the next best thing is to use the water from your tap, however city water often has added chemicals like chlorine or fluoride.

To get these chemicals out and to add more beneficial bacteria in, get a bucket of water and let it sit for at least 24 hours (the longer the better). The chemicals evaporate and the bacteria which are beneficial to plants begin to grow.

The only downside to letting the water sit is that it becomes stagnant (lack of oxygen in the water).

A quick way to add the air back into the water is to pour the water through a screen or sieve. Doing this before you water Tulsi will help Her greatly with being happy and healthy.

Transplanting

When transplanting Tulsi make sure you have bought the correct type and size of pot for Her, for the next weeks or months (depending on Her growth rate). See section Pot Size and Type for more information.

This is an example of a Tulsi that needs to be transplanted

The first sign Tulsi needs a bigger pot is if Her roots are coming out of the drainage hole at the bottom of the pot. However, this may not always be the case as Her roots might be blocked by the stone or piece of pot you placed over the drainage hole. The second sign is how She looks. Is the visible part of Tulsi 3/4 or more of Her entire size (including Her roots)? If the answer is Yes, probably a good time to transplant Her.

Transplanting Tulsi is very easy and enjoyable. Here are some tips to help you in moving Her to a bigger pot.

1. Plan to transplant Tulsi in the shade or on a cloudy day.

2. Slightly water Tulsi before taking Her out of Her smaller pot. The water will help the soil stick together making the migration easier and less messy.

3. Place a stone or a piece of a broken flower pot over the drainage hole of the new pot.

4. Fill the new pot with soil leaving a hole in the middle about the dimensions of the soil from the smaller pot.

5. Carefully loosen the soil around the edges of the old pot with a garden trowel. Pick up the pot, hold Tulsi in your arm and gently pull out the soil. Place Tulsi inside the new pot, being careful not to heavily damage Her roots.

6. Pay close attention not to fill the pot too full of soil, as when you water Tulsi the water may overflow. Also make sure the tops of the old soil and new soil are flat. Add or subtract soil as needed.

7. Water Tulsi until the water is coming out the drainage hole. The air pockets in the soil will be released. Add more soil. Make sure to allow Her soil to fully dry out before watering Her again.

8. Keep Tulsi in the shade for the rest of the day. Transplanting can be a shock to Her. If She looks a bit wilty for a day or two, or Her growth speed decreases for some days, it is normal. Do not worry.

Lighting

Tulsi Devi will enjoy as much direct sunlight as She can get. If you have the perfect place where Tulsi can get 8 to 10 hours (of course depending on the year) of sunlight She will do great. It is important to note that direct sunlight is not the same as indirect sunlight. This may seem to be common sense, however having Tulsi in a naturally bright room is not the same as having Her outside in direct sunlight. Tulsi needs direct light, either from the sun or from an artificial light source.

Grow Lights

The first and most important thing in growing Tulsi indoors is lighting. From the perspective of the plant (not visual aesthetics) there are three major things one needs to look at when deciding on which lights to get: Colour frequency, Watts (or amount of energy; not lumens), and amount of time the lights need to be on.

Colour Frequency

Not any old light will do. Actually if one chooses an incorrect type of light Tulsi can even become sick. Why? Because the colour of the light is wrong. Most light we see indoors are yellow or red. Having only these colours will not help Tulsi grow healthily.

Colour Tempertures in the Kelvin Scale

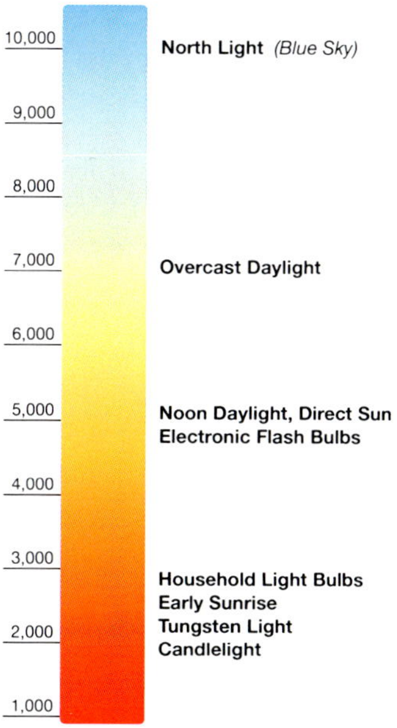

The two main colours of grow lights: Red and Blue. The colour of the light is based on the temperature of the light; red being cold and blue being hot. The degrees of temperature are measured in Kelvins (K).

Red: Red coloured lights (1000K to 4000K [red coloured lights also include yellow frequency, such as normal incandescent lights]) are perfect for flowering plants or plants that you want to be put into their flowering stages. Tulsi is not one of these. Especially in the winter, it is important that She does not waste energy on flowers and seeds.

Prolonged exposure to the red lights will make Tulsi grow tall and weak with little leaves.

Blue: Blue coloured lights (5000K+) are perfect for salads, spinach, basil (Tulsi) and other herbs where their main 'crop' is their leaves. The Blue Lights help create photosynthesis; this helps Tulsi grow strong and stocky with many leaves.

Watts

In most cases when we look at the wattage of a bulb we think about how much light it will create (which is measured in lumens). Of course in most cases (e.g. offices, bedrooms, bathrooms) we care most about the lumens as we do not want the room to be too bright or too dark. However when it comes to growing plants, lumens mean almost nothing, as the amount of brightness is not what makes the plants do photosynthesis, it is the energy inside the light (which can be measured in watts).

With artificial light there is a law, called the Inverse-square Law, which states that the amount of energy diminishes exponentially as the distance from the source increases. This is the equation: for every 12 inches (≈ 30 cm) the power decreases by half. So if Tulsi is 24 inches (≈ 60 cm) tall the amount of energy reaching the base of Tulsi is only 25% of the original watts.

To keep Tulsi healthy it is suggested to have at least 50 watts per square foot (30 cm) per hour; however it is actually 50 watts per cubic foot per hour as Tulsi is three dimensional.

Note: if the plant is 24 inches tall and you are using only one 50 watt bulb, the amount of energy reaching the base of the plant will only be 12.5 watts. This is not good. There is a simple way to supplement the loss in energy; add light reflectors, such as white boards or aluminum foil that reflects the light back up to the plant from below. This is not the best solution but it is cheap and it does help. The best solution however, would be to place more lights around Tulsi vertically pointing at Her from the side.

Amount of Artificial Daylight

If you live in a climate that doesn't allow Tulsi to live outside all year around, you will need to bring Her inside during the winter. Making sure She has adequate amount of light is very important. To sustain Tulsi throughout the winter so in the spring time She can be happily put outside as soon as possible. If this is your goal, 12 to 14 hours of light is adequate.

This Tulsi is four times larger than Her sisters, which were germinated on the same day. The difference is that this Tulsi has received adequate artificial lighting.

With that said, you can also happily grow a very healthy Tulsi Devi in a room which has little to no direct Sunlight (maybe your temple or meditation room) all year around. If this is what you desire, you will only need to make sure She is getting enough artificial light (50 watts per 12 cubic inches [30 cubic cm] and 14 to 18 hours of light).

To help you keep track of how many hours of light Tulsi is getting it is important to get a timer. This will also help you make sure the light is turned on and off at the same time each day (this is important for Tulsi's overall health).

It is also helpful to turn Her light off two to three times a day for 15 to 30 mins at a time. These resting periods will support Her growth and Her overall health.

It is important to note that if your Tulsi is not able to get enough sunlight even in summer time, add a grow light next to Her. The grow light can and should be on even during the day when Tulsi is getting direct sunlight. The grow light will not interfere with the natural sunlight, it will only add to it.

The last point to be aware of is how Tulsi grows towards the light. You will see when your Tulsi is very young She will bend very fast and to a large degree toward Her light source. Make sure to turn Her at least 90 degrees once day. If possible you can turn Her more often and place a stick next to Her inside the soil and gently tie Her to it, so that She has something to brace up against as She grows. This will help Her grow happy and healthy.

Temperature

Tulsi prefers to have it 50F (10C) or warmer. She even enjoys it when it gets into the 90s F (30s C). However when it becomes this warm, make sure Tulsi is not being left too long in the direct sun, as it may burn Her, and make sure She is getting enough water.

Tulsi can be okay as low as 40F (4C) however if it stays this cold for too long, Her growth will be stunted.

Tulsi should never be left outside if it is freezing (32F, 0C). The frost will damage Her, and it may even kill Her.

Tulsi likes it to be warm all year around. If you live in a climate that doesn't allow Tulsi to live outside all year around, you must bring Her inside and keep the room She is in at a comfortable temperature (50F+, 10C+).

Humidity

Tulsi prefers it not to be too dry. If you live in an area where it is very dry, you will need to watch your Tulsi. She may become dry even with adequate water in Her soil. To support a humid environment, mist Tulsi once or twice a day. This will help create a micro climate around Her. Also when multiple Tulsis are placed together, they will benefit from each other's perspiration.

If none of this works, place Tulsi in a greenhouse and spray the floor with water. The heat will make the water evaporate, creating a humid climate. If it begins to steam, it is too hot so you will need to create some type of ventilation *(e.g. open doors or windows)*. When steam is a constant problem, spray the floor at night and leave the doors and windows open during the day.

Air Quality

Tulsi prefers to be in a space where the air is fresh (or at least able to be exchanged once or twice a day). Also it is important to have a gentle breeze passing by Tulsi every so often during the day. Plants need to breathe, but they do not have lungs which can force air to move for them. A small oscillating fan would do the trick.

Pruning and Taking leaves form Tulsi

In general we must remember Tulsi is a Goddess, not a mere plant. Pruning Her or taking Her leaves must be done with care and with purpose.

This young flower spike can be picked with your finger nails.

Tulsi will spend much of Her energy on growing new flowers (manjaris) not in growing new leaves and branches. This is okay, however She will become weak in times of stress (eg changing of seasons or changing of living area). She may also become tall with few leaves.

To prevent this pinch the new flower spikes off with your fingers once you can see them. If the flower spikes are too hard to do it with your fingernails, than you may use a scissors. Remember to prune Tulsi with love and care.

The only time it is acceptable to prune full branches is if the branch is already completely dry or if it will directly save Her life. Other than these two reasons, never prune full branches off Tulsi.

When the flower spikes have fully grown, you may need a scissors.

If your Tulsi is healthy enough, you may pick leaves from Her with your fingernails for two reasons: 1. Prayer 2. Medicinal

Remember to also pick Her leaves with love and caring, and ask Her for permission, first. She will always say, "Yes."

Pests

It is almost certain that Tulsi will get some type of pest, which in and of itself is a mystery.

Tulsi is known to be, when ingested, an antiparasitic; like cayenne peppers or neem. However the mysterious part is, cayenne peppers and neem are antiparasitic all the time, when ingested or not. Small insects do not eat these plants, yet they eat Tulsi?

This shows Tulsi is not a normal plant and should not be treated as such. It also shows Her unconditional Love for Her children. Two reasons:

1. She is willing to literally allow Herself to be eaten to death for the sake of the health of these insects. By them being on Her and eating Her, they for sure will be liberated from that level of existence. Such is Her Grace.

2. The pests are there because Tulsi is also taking karma from the one who is caring for Her. This is Her duty and Her greatest joy. She is willing to do anything just to know that Her children can get one step closer to the Divine.

Does that mean we should not help Her when She is ill? Of course not. By doing our best is helping Her, She will be even more pleased and help us get closer to the Divine.

The best way to keep the pests to a minimum is to be proactive in preventing them. Here are some tips:

1. Buy good quality soil from a reputable company. This will decrease the chances of having insect eggs hitchhike in the soil.

2. Finely mist Tulsi once or twice a day. This will help create a micro climate around Tulsi that will help discourage pest (especially whitefly and spidermites). Do this before or after Her light source is on Her. The beads of water can magnify the light and burn Her leaves.

3. Gently wash Tulsi with water once a week.

Whiteflies

Whiteflies are amongst the most prevalent pests, and they seem to L-O-V-E Tulsi. The best way to combat Whiteflies is to be preventative. Whiteflies are attracted to greenish-yellow colours (exactly Tulsi's colours). By placing one or more sticky yellow cards around Tulsi (the best place is slightly above Her) the whiteflies will go there, stick and die (yes, for the sake of Tulsi it is okay to kill; She will take the karma).

Whiteflies live on the underside of Tulsi's leaves.

If Tulsi does have whiteflies, the easiest way to keep them in check is to gently wash Her leaves with a little organic, soft soap. Place a drop or two of soap into a bucket of lukewarm water.

Whiteflies lay their eggs on the underside of leaves. If you see white dots, these are the eggs. Gently rub them off. If they firmly stick, use your fingernail, however, be careful not to hurt Her.

After washing Tulsi with soap and water, if She has a lot of suds on Her leaves, gently rinse Her with water. The soap may burn Her leaves. If not, you may let Her air dry.

To make sure you get them all, wash Tulsi once every 5 to 7 days for 3 to 4 weeks.

When you gently shake Tulsi and if you see a small cloud of whiteflies coming off Her, then the whitefly population has gotten too large. Go to your local gardening shop and buy some whitefly poison. Talk to the gardening shop and look for a poison that can be used on edible plants. These tend not to be damaging to Tulsi.

Aphids

Aphids are small insects that often live on leaves and stems of Tulsi. They drink Her sap.

Like whiteflies, Aphis can be dealt with by washing with a soft organic soap (see whitefly for instructions on how to wash Tulsi). They can also be blasted off by a squirt of a water bottle. Be careful not to damage Tulsi's leaves.

The green dots are aphids and the black dots are dead whitefly eggs.

Watch out for aphids as they can reproduce very fast. Even one is enough. If you see an aphid, wash Tulsi as soon as possible.

If the aphid population gets out of control, it can kill Her. If washing Tulsi is not enough, go to your local gardening center and get a product that is good for basil and works against aphids.

Spidermites

Spidermites are often hard to detect until their population has spread all around Tulsi. They seem to colonize primarily on her flower spikes coating them with webs. If not controlled spidermites can kill Tulsi.

The best way to deal with spidermites is to gently mist Tulsi once or twice a day. Spidermites find it difficult to hang on to wet stems and leaves so they will search out dry plants.

Secondly, washing Tulsi with soap and water will help (see whitefly for instructions on how to wash Tulsi). If it doesn't cure Her pest problem then go to your local gardening shop and buy a miticide. If possible buy one that is made for edible plants.

Soil Gnats

Soil gnats are small black flies that can often been seen walking on the top of the soil or flying around Tulsi. The adult flies do nothing to harm Tulsi, but the larvae can. The larvae eat organic material which can include Tulsi's roots. A few soil gnats is not much of a problem, however if the population gets out of control the larvae can even kill Tulsi.

Soil gnats love wet soil. Allowing the soil to fully dry out will give the soil gnats a reason to leave. If possible put Tulsi outside during the day; the soil gnats may fly away.

Do not give Tulsi new soil. The fresh organic material will fuel the population growth.

In the worst case scenario, buy soil gnat poison. There are some types of poison that are completely benign to Tulsi but do help get rid of the soil gnat.

Fungi in the Soil

Fungi or mushrooms can be found in Tulsi's soil if Her soil is constantly damp and She is kept in a cool place. Sometimes the fungi or mushrooms will grow on the top of the soil. If so, gently take away the top layer of Tulsi's soil, being careful not to damage Her roots. Replace with fresh soil.

However, you cannot always see the fungus. At times it can also be in the soil attacking Her roots.

To prevent a fungi problem keep Tulsi in a warm room. Do not over water and at times, to make sure all the water has left the pot, you may refrain from watering Her for an extended amount of time. She will begin to wilt slightly. This is okay. Once you have watered Her, within 20 mins to 30 mins She will be perking right back up.

See the section on patting Tulsi for more information about preferred pot size and type.

Changing of Seasons

When the seasons change Tulsi might lose leaves as the amount and time of sunlight change, She will need new leaves that are accustomed to that time of year. Do not worry if this happens, it is normal.

What to do when Tulsi leaves Her body

Tulsi will die. It is normal and it is natural. If you have done your best to take care of Her, it is Her will She left. Do not worry, plant another Tulsi when you are ready.

You may bury your old Tulsi, or place Her in a river or a stream. Once Her branches are dry, you may make malas out of the wood, or offer them in a yagna ceremony. Whatever you choose, do it with respect and love; She will be very grateful.

benefits of caring for tulsi devi

The benefits Tulsi happily throws upon the one who cares for Her are literally infinite. These benefits range from health of the body to moksha (liberation) and everywhere in between.

Health Benefits

Tulsi is a wonder drug. The amount of health benefits are so many that it is difficult to write them all down and more benefits are being found every day.

When ingested or placed on the body, Tulsi is:

1. Antibacterial
2. Antifungal
3. Antiviral
4. Antiparasitic
5. High in iron
6. High in antioxidants
7. High in stress reducing chemicals
8. Blood cleansing
9. Digestion improving
10. Gas reducing
11. Cholesterol reducing
12. Immune system boosting
13. Headache and body pain relieving
14. Fever reducing
15. Blood pressure regulating
16. Blood sugar level regulating
17. Vitamin C and A containing
18. Zinc containing
19. Memory and concentration improving

These are only a few health benefits Tulsi is known for. Tulsi is completely safe and it has been recommended by some ayurvedic doctors to take up to 20 – 25 Tulsi leaves twice a day. This may be a bit excessive, but it shows that Tulsi is the only ayurvedic plant that has no maximum limit.

Of course, consult your doctor to see if Tulsi is safe for you, however for most, Tulsi is only beneficial.

Remember to at least mentally offer the Tulsi leaves or tea to the Divine before you ingest Her. This will please Her immensely.

As you begin to care for Tulsi you will see that She is not a normal plant. Her willingness to be used for medicinal use demonstrates Her Motherly Love. It is not like being plucked and then dunked into boiling water doesn't hurt. Yet Tulsi is ever ready to suffer for the benefit of Her children.

Spiritual Benefits

The benefits one receives spiritually for caring for Tulsi are remarkable. In Her life as the queen of Sankhschuda, Tulsi was the epitome of faith and bhakti (Love for the Divine). It takes such faith and bhakti to have self-realization, and Tulsi gives it happily and freely to Her children. The best and foremost benefit of caring for Tulsi is true, pure bhakti for the Divine (any form you feel close to).

To do this Tulsi continuously purifies Her caretaker by taking karma from them, onto Herself. By simply looking at Tulsi, She takes karma. By simply watering Tulsi, She takes karma. By simply misting Tulsi, She takes karma. By simply washing Tulsi, She takes karma. By simply planting or transplanting Tulsi, She takes karma. By simply touching Tulsi, She takes karma. By simply taking the soil from which Tulsi is planted in as prasad, She takes karma. By simply ingesting Her leaves or flowers, She takes karma. By simply praying to Tulsi, She takes karma. By simply talking about Tulsi, She takes karma. By simply listening to stories of Tulsi, She takes karma. By simply bowing down to Tulsi, She takes karma. By simply thinking of Tulsi, She takes karma.

And most importantly, by simply offering one of Her leaves or flowers to the Divine, She will bless you with more grace and love than you can imagine. At the same time the form of the Divine you offered Her to, will be extremely pleased with you, as Tulsi (Bhakti Itself) has been offered to Them. Tulsi, with Her endless bhakti, intercedes for us, and asks the Divine to accept this small leaf as if it has been offered by a saint. With so much sweetness and mercy, how can the Divine say no?

Even though bhakti is the most important benefit, Tulsi also freely blesses Her caretakers with anything they desire, e.g. wealth, children, husband, wife, good job, knowledge. All the Devas and Devis dwell with Her, so She has the power to give absolutely anything.

When one has Tulsi in their home, all negative vastu (or feng-shui) is immediately destroyed. Tulsi protects the home and those who live within it from all sorts of negativity. Negativity from others, negative entities and even Death Itself runs from Tulsi. That is also why we wear Tulsi kunti malas (small beaded necklaces) around our neck. She protects us from all negativity.

Having Tulsi in the home will ensure a peaceful and loving atmosphere to raise children and have a family.

If one has children, try to have them support in taking care of Tulsi, even if it is only misting Her once a day. She will bless them, helping them with their schooling. As the Vedas dwell within Her, She is the store house of all knowledge and wisdom, too.

Tulsi is the only puja paraphernalia that can be offered more than once; Tulsi can be offered infinite amount of times. As She is purity incarnate, She can never become impure no matter what has touched Her or where She has been.

Tulsi is the sweetest of the sweet. The kindest of the kind. The wisest of the wise. And the most merciful of the merciful. Never doubt Her ever-willingness to help Her children. She will always be with those who look after Her.

What one can learn by observing Tulsi

If we observe Tulsi we can learn so many important lessons of how we should live our life.

Firstly we can observe Tulsi's humility. She is the Queen of the Universe and yet She happily lives in a pot of soil. If the Queen of queens is content living in soil, then shouldn't we be content with what Divine has given to us?

Next we can observe Her unyielding positivity. We can neglect Tulsi and not water Her, or wash Her, or pay much attention to Her for some time, yet once we do, She is immediately thrilled and throws boons at us. If Tulsi has not been watered in some days, She will be wilty and sickly; yet once we water Her, in no time at all She will be upright and healthy again. The same is for when She is has many pests and yet we do not wash Her. She will become sickly, but once we wash Her, it almost appears that She has gotten a new life. If Tulsi can so quickly forgive and forget our insults to Her, than should we not do the same to others?

We can also see the importance of perseverance. Tulsi can become very sick and lose even 99% of Her leaves, and yet, if there is still one leaf left, there is hope that She will grow back. This has happened many times. Tulsi is Bhakti and Faith, and if, like Her we can in the worst of times have just a bit of faith, we will see once the time is right ,our bhakti will grow back stronger and more plentiful than ever before. Like Tulsi, we must never give up.

Tulsi also shows us that life is transitory. The world is not eternal and nor are we. Tulsi who is eternal, mystically incarnates, grows, suffers and then dies, going back to the Lord. If we fix our minds on the Divine, just like Tulsi, we will be non-attached to this world and its mediocre pleasures. Surrendering ourselves to the Divine we will find the true everlasting happiness inside our hearts.

Tulsi is the perfect example of one who constantly sacrifices for others. Tulsi happily allows Herself to be plucked and eaten for the betterment of Her children. We can also see that She sees everyone and everything equally with the same Divine Love. Not only does She sacrifice Herself for us humans, She will also happily die for animals and insects too. If the Mother of all is willing to die for us, can't we also sacrifice a bit or ourselves for Her and for Her children?

And ultimately we see the never ending joy of sacrificing Herself to be close to Her Lord and God, Narayana. Nothing makes Tulsi happier than to be placed at the feet of Her Lord. Of course to be placed there Her leaves need to be plucked off; She needs to go through physical pain, yet with no second thoughts, She joyfully does it. If Tulsi can happily lose Her limbs to be closer to the Divine, can't we learn to sacrifice just a bit of ourselves to be closer to our Devata, too?

Tulsi is the perfect example of a true bhakta of the Divine. If we take these few examples to heart and implement them into our lives, our path to self-realization will be completely ensured.

tulsī puja

This simple puja was placed in this booklet, as an offering, if you would like to also care for Tulsi in this way.

01 *Wash your hands, say:*
om apa upa sprasya

02 *Pranams (fold your hands, greet TulsiDevi and chant three times):*
om yanmule sarva thirthāni
yanmadye sarva devathā
yadagre sarva vedashchā
tulsi twām namāmayham

03 *Asanam (offer flower petal):*
om sri tulsi devyai namaha
āsanam samarpayāmi

04 *Asking permission to do Puja (offer flower petal):*
om sri tulsi devyai namaha
asmin ārādhana karmani anumanyathām

05 *Wash Her symbolically (sprinkle some drops of water on Her, and wash Her pot of kumkum and chandan):*
om sri tulsi devyai namaha
snapayāmi

06 *Dry Her symbolically (offer a flower petal):*
om sri tulsi devyai namaha
plodham samarpayāmi

07 *Clothes (offer flower petals to symbolically dress Her):*
om sri tulsi devyai namaha
vastram samarpayāmi

08 *Upper clothes (offer flower petals):*
om sri tulsi devyai namaha
utharēyam samarpayāmi

09 *Jewellery (offer flower petals):*
om sri tulsi devyai namaha
ābaranam samarpayāmi

10 *Chandan (apply one dot on Her pot):*
om sri tulsi devyai namaha
chandanam samarpayāmi

11 *Kumkum (apply one dot on Her pot):*
om sri tulsi devyai namaha
kumkumam samarpayāmi

12 *Flower:*
om sri tulsi devyai namaha
sugandha pushpam samarpayāmi

13 *Perfume (apply on a flower which you offer to Her):*
om sri tulsi devyai namaha
dravyam samarpayaami

14 *Dhoopam-incense stick (ring bell):*
om sri tulsi devyai namaha
dhoopam dhoopayāmi

15 *Drink (offer a small portion of water into Her soil, ring bell):*
om sri tulsi devyai namaha
pānēyam samarpayāmi

16 *Food (offer Her food, ring bell):*
om sri tulsi devyai namaha
nivedhayām samarpayāmi

17 *Deepam (put a small clay lamp filled with oil in front of Her, ring bell):*
om sri tulsi devyai namaha
deepam samarpayāmi

18 *Offer akshata or flower petal:*
om sri tulsi devyai namaha
asanādhi samasta upacharan samarpayami

19 *Pradakshina Mantra (circumambulate Tulsi Devi three times clockwise and chant the Pradakshina Mantra with each circumambulation):*
yani kani cha pāpani
brahma-hatyadikani cha
tani tani prana shanti
pradakshinaha pade pade

19 *Aarti (small Aarti, ring bell, chant three times Her Gayatri):*
om tulsi devyai cha vidmahe
vishnu priyayai dhēmahi
thanno tulsi prachodayāth

tulsi devi ashtottara shatanamavali

01 om sri tulasee-devyai namaha
02 om sri sakhyai namaha
03 om sri bhadrayai namaha
04 om sri mano gynana pallavayai namaha
05 om puranda rasatee pujyayai namaha
06 om punyadayai namaha
07 om punya rupinyai namaha
08 om jynana vigynana jananyai namaha
09 om tatva gyna priyayai namaha
10 om jaanakee dukha shamanyai namaha
11 om janardhana prayayai namaha
12 om sarva kalmasha samhartyai namaha
13 om smara koti sama prabhayai namaha
14 om panchalee pujya charanayai namaha
15 om paparanya davanalayai namaha
16 om kami tardha pradayai namaha
17 om gouree sharada samsevitayai namaha
18 om vandaru jana manda rayai namaha
19 om nilimpa bharana saktayai namaha
20 om lakshmi chandra sahodaryai namaha
21 om sanakadi munidye yayai namaha
22 om krushna nanda janitryai namaha
23 om chida nanda svarupenyai namaha
24 om narayanyai namaha
25 om satya rupayai namaha
26 om maya teetayai namaha

27 om mahe shvaryai namaha
28 om shubha pradayai namaha
29 om vadanacha vinirdhu taraka purnani shakarayai namaha
30 om rochana panka tilakala sannitala bhasurayai namaha
31 om shudhayai namaha
32 om palla vostyai namaha
33 om padma mukyai namaha
34 om pulla padma dale kshanayai namaha
35 om champe yakali kakaranasa danda viraji tayai namaha
36 om mandas mitayai namaha
37 om manjulangyai namaha
38 om madhava priya bhamenyai namaha
39 om manikya kankana dharayai namaha
40 om mani kundala manditayai namaha
41 om indra sampatka rtyai namaha
42 om shaktyai namaha
43 om indra gopa nibhamshu kayai namaha
44 om kshirabdhi tana yayai namaha
45 om kshira sagara samkshi vayai namaha
46 om shanti kanti guno petayai namaha
47 om brundanu guna samptryai namaha
48 om putāt mekayai namaha
49 om puta nadi svarupenyai namaha
50 om yoga dyeyayai namaha
51 om yoga nanda padayai namaha
52 om chatur varga pradayai namaha
53 om chaturvarna eika pavanayai namaha
54 om triloka jananyai namaha
55 om gruhamedhi samaradhyayai namaha
56 om sada namgana pavanayai namaha
57 om muneendra hrudaya vasayai namaha
58 om mula prakruti sangyni kayai namaha

59 om bramha rupinyai namaha
60 om param jyotishyai namaha
61 om avajana sago charayai namaha
62 om pancha bhutatmi kayai namaha
63 om panchakalat mikayai namaha
64 om yogayai namaha
65 om achyu tayai namaha
66 om yagyna rupinyai namaha
67 om samsara dukha shamanyai namaha
68 om srushti sthityamta karinyai namaha
69 om sarva prapamcha nirmatryai namaha
70 om vaishnavyai namaha
71 om madhura svarupayai namaha
72 om nireesvarayai namaha
73 om nirgunayai namaha
74 om nityayai namaha
75 om niratamkayai namaha
76 om dīna jana palana tatparayai namaha
77 om ranatkimkineekajala ratna kancheela satkatayai namaha
78 om chalanmamjeera charanayai namaha
79 om chaturana sevitayai namaha
80 om ahoratra karinyai namaha
81 om mukta hara bhara krantayai namaha
82 om mudrika ratna bhasurayai namaha
83 om sidhi pradayai namaha
84 om amalāyai namaha
85 om kamalāyai namaha
86 om loka sundaryai namaha
87 om hema kumbha kuchadva yayai namaha
88 om lasita kumbha chadva yayai namaha
89 om chancha laayai namaha
90 om lakshmyai namaha
91 om sri krushna priyayai namaha
92 om rama priyayai namaha

93 om vishnu priyayai namaha
94 om shankaryai namaha
95 om shiva shankaryai namaha
96 om kunda kutma laradanayai namaha
97 om pakva bimboshryai namaha
98 om shara shchandri kayai namaha
99 om champe yanasi kayai namaha
100 om kanbu sundara galayai namaha
101 om tatilla tangyai namaha
102 om matta bandhura kunta layai namaha
103 om nakshatra nibhana khayai namaha
104 om rambhani bhoru yugmayai namaha
105 om saikata shronyai namaha
106 om madakanti rava madyayai namaha
107 om keera vanyai namaha
108 om srī mahā tulasyāi namaha

om tulsi devyai cha vidmahe
vishnu priyayai dhimahi
thanno tulsi prachodayath